JESUS CHRIST, YESTERDAY, TODAY AND FOR EVER

A SERIES OF STUDIES FOR THE MILLENNIUM

BY
ELFED AP NEFYDD ROBERTS

Published on behalf of
The Presbyterian Church of Wales
by Gwasg Pantycelyn Caernarfon

Design - StrataMatrix

The Presbyterian Church of Wales,
53 Richmond Road, Cardiff CF2 3UP

CONTENTS

	Page
Introduction by the Moderator of the General Assembly	05
Preface	08

Jesus Christ Yesterday

Study 1:	Jesus the Man	11
Study 2:	Jesus the Prophet	17
Study 3:	Jesus the Healer	23
Study 4:	Jesus the Servant	31

Jesus Christ Today

Study 5:	Jesus, Son of God	39
Study 6:	Jesus the Saviour	47
Study 7:	Jesus the Lord	55
Study 8:	Jesus the Way	63

Jesus Christ for Ever

Study 9:	Jesus, Head of the Church	69
Study 10:	The Cosmic Christ	77
Study 11:	Christ the Judge	87
Study 12:	Christ, Alpha and Omega	95

Sources	102

© The Presbyterian Church of Wales

ISBN 1 874786 92 5

All rights reserved. No part of this book may be reproduced or transmitted in any form or by any means, electronic or mechanical, including photocopying, recording, or by any information storage and retrieval system, without permission in writing from the publisher.

The publishers acknowledge the support of the
Welsh Books Council

Published by Gwasg Pantycelyn, Caernarfon on behalf of
the Presbyterian Church of Wales. Printed in Wales.

INTRODUCTION
By the Moderator of the General Assembly

It was in a meeting of the General Assembly Department that the author of this volume suggested the words "Jesus Christ, the same Yesterday, Today and Forever" (Hebrews 13:8) as the motto of our Connexion as we move towards the Millennium. He would hardly have thought at the time that he would be invited to prepare these studies for us, as he left the Theological College where he had been training our candidates in pastoral work, in order to recommence that work himself with the large church at Capel y Groes, Wrexham.

I am sure that it was not an easy task to complete a volume of this kind during that period of change. But with his great experience as a minister and teacher, as an author and a preacher, no-one more suitable could have been found to lead us with Jesus Christ to the gates of the new century.

I know that our former Principal has been a wise director on many committees and a number of panels and as an acknowledged historian, an enlightened communicator and a man learned in the doctrines we could not choose anyone with a more safe and balanced opinion to lead our thoughts past yesterday and today, with thanks, to the tomorrow of our risen Lord.

In our century with thousands of books and articles having been published about Jesus of Nazareth, it would be easy to drown in the deep waters. Christology (the study of the Person of Christ) can tempt some to stir the waters, sometimes deliberately, on other occasions not so deliberately. This happened frequently after Dietrich Bonhoeffer asked the question that he was not allowed to live to answer fully; "Who is Jesus Christ to us today?" Others in the second half of this century went to answer the question "from below" and they concentrated on "Jesus the Man", in other words "the human face of God". Professor John Macquarrie attempted to keep safe the paradox which is to be found in many of Ann

The Reverend W.I.Cynwil Williams B.A., B.D.

Griffiths' hymns and at the same time keeping quiet those more conservative theologians who insist on beginning "from above".

Before this the discussion on the Person of Christ had stirred the waters in our own Courts. The unfortunate episode of the excommunication of Peter Williams of Carmarthen happened very early in the history of the Connexion. Closer to our own days again in the Tywi Valley, Tom Nefyn Williams appeared before the Association and he was also excommunicated. A number of volumes have been written on Christology including several Davies Lectures but by now it has become a subject to avoid as we dare not upset the apple cart! But with the future of mankind in the balance we must listen to all views, the conservative, liberal, the political and the radical. The distress of the world is bound to bring us together and the One who has asked us to follow him is far too great to be wounded by blinkered people.

Some years ago a request reached Dr. Hans-Ruedi Weber for a volume similar to this one. He decided to write about Jesus under the titles: The Artist, the Sage and the Crucified. He could see that these titles would appeal to people's imagination and to venture, to take part in God's work in the world and, obeying him to protect our world and its people in order to restore the creation in the name of Jesus who regularly takes us into God's presence.

The Revd Elfed ap Nefydd Roberts has used to a great extent the works of the artists and has spanned, without making it obvious the judgement of the different theologians about Jesus Christ. Since he is familiar with the classical language of the Church throughout the centuries and is a master at giving his meditations a devotional feeling, he has made a notable literary contribution as always. This volume will be very useful and where there will be sensible instruction it will be a volume to promote Christian philanthropy and world wide mission. In a word it fosters far reaching worship and understanding of the thought of Jesus, the Christ.

W.I. Cynwil Williams

PREFACE

The main significance of the turn of the Millennium is that it marks the coming of Jesus Christ into our world two thousand years ago. But we do more than simply acknowledge a historical fact. We affirm and celebrate the formative contribution of the religion of Christ to our world and our civilization. The example, teaching and influence of Jesus gave to humanity its highest values and noblest ideals. And if the story of the Christian Church has not always been spotless and guiltless, most often the reason for its failure was that it lost sight of Jesus and allowed wealth, worldly power, superstition or oppressive orthodoxy to usurp the place which was his alone. And if our religious life and witness today are feeble and ineffective, could it not be that the main reason for our failure is that we too have lost sight of the wonder and the radical challenge of Jesus Christ?

As the Millennium is above all else the birthday of Jesus, it was resolved to adopt as a theme for our celebrations as a Church the familiar words of the Letter to the Hebrews: *'Jesus Christ is the same yesterday, today and for ever'* (Hebrews 13:8). The purpose of this series of studies is to help church and house groups to address the question, Who is Jesus Christ for us today? It is suggested that the studies should be used between September and December in preparation for the turn of the Millennium. The first four studies, entitled *Jesus Christ Yesterday*, consider who Jesus was to his contemporaries, under the headings Jesus the Man, Jesus the Prophet, Jesus the Healer and Jesus the Servant. The four studies which follow deal with *Jesus Christ Today*, under the headings, Jesus, Son of God, Jesus the Saviour, Jesus the Lord, and Jesus the Way. Aspects of the person and work of Christ yet to be fully realized in the future are considered under *Jesus Christ for Ever*, namely, Christ, Head of the Church, The Cosmic Christ, Christ the Judge, and Christ, Alpha and Omega.

The studies give attention not only to the biblical foundations of each of these topics but also to the interpretations and insights of more recent writers, poets and artists. Art has always played a central role within the Christian tradition and alongside each study is a portrayal of Christ by either a traditional or contemporary artist.

Following a brief devotional opening (a hymn and short prayer), the leader of the group should give a short summary of the introduction before turning to the Bible study material. In order to encourage the participation of as many as possible within the group, arrangements should be made beforehand for different members to read the designated verses of scripture, quotations and prayers. Should the group consist of more than twelve members it would be of advantage to divide into smaller groupings of about six to discuss the questions and the pictures and then to report briefly to the whole gathering before the meeting concludes with a time of prayer and a final hymn.

It is hoped that these studies will be a means of encouraging exploration into the majesty and mystery of Christ, in order that we may, in the words of Richard of Chichester, 'see him more clearly, love him more dearly, follow him more nearly,' and walk confidently into the Third Millennium in his company and his strength.

Jesus Christ Yesterday

STUDY 1

JESUS THE MAN

AIM
To consider the human elements in the person of Jesus, particularly those aspects of his personality which made the first impact upon his contemporaries, and to consider the significance of his humanness for our Christian faith and life today.

WELCOME AND OPENING DEVOTIONS
Hymn: *'O Son of Man, our Hero strong and tender,'* (C.H. 309) followed by a short opening prayer.

STARTING POINT
The opening hymn by Frank Fletcher centres on the humanness of Jesus, his strength and tenderness, and his identification with our sorrows and joys. At the same time, he is *Son of Man, King and Lord*. Christian faith states that Jesus is fully man as well as fully God and that his humanity and his divinity must always be held together in balance.

It should not surprise us that the contemporaries of Jesus saw him first and foremost as a man. But the extraordinary quality of his humanness led some to believe that he was also more than an ordinary human being. Similarly, we today see the divine-human glory of Jesus by recognizing, first of all, the quality of his humanness. Unless we begin with Jesus the man, there is a danger that traditional and age-old images and concepts will prevent us from discovering the real Jesus. That is the danger of which we are warned in Meirion Evan's poem, *I Believe*.[1]

Jesus Christ Yesterday

...What shall we do
with the pansy Christ
who hangs high
on the walls of the memories' vestries?
We shall tear
the petticoat that is about him
so that we can see the eternal arms
all hair and muscles
and the hands like shovels
whipping synod and government.
Under the dirt marks
of the inquisitive fingers of the years
and the vestry and the vatican's
layers of old varnish,
is the original portrait
of the Artisan from Nazareth...

Is it possible that our image of Christ is unreal, the product of imagination and fantasy? Is the poet right in assuming that the original picture is that of the 'Artisan from Nazareth'?

BIBLE STUDY

At many points in the New Testament Jesus is referred to as a *man*.

When John the Baptist saw Jesus approaching, he said "This is he of whom I said, 'After me comes a man who ranks ahead of me because he was before me." (John 1:30).

Similarly, the woman of Samaria said to the people of the city, "Come and see a man who told me everything I have ever done! He cannot be the Messiah, can he?" (John 4: 29).

John's Gospel gives us the account of Pilate leading Jesus out before the crowd:

Jesus Christ Yesterday

'So Jesus came out, wearing the crown of thorns and the purple robe. Pilate said to them, "Here is the man!" (John 19:5).

In his first recorded sermon in Jerusalem on the Day of Pentecost, Peter declared,

'"You that are Israelites, listen to what I have to say: Jesus of Nazareth, a man attested to you by God with deeds of power, wonders and signs that God did through him among you, as you yourselves know – this man, handed over to you ... you crucified and killed by the hands of those outside the law."' (Acts 2: 22-23).

In speaking of the role of Jesus as mediator between God and man, the First Letter to Timothy refers to the humanity of Jesus:

'For there is one God; there is also one mediator between God and humankind, Christ Jesus, himself human.' (1 Timothy 2:5)

In each of the above examples Jesus is referred to either as *man* or as *a man* – both terms being translations of two Greek words, one of which means a specific male member of the human race, and the other *man* as a representative of humanity in general. In both senses, those who knew Jesus in the flesh declared him to be fully and naturally human.

At the same time his humanness is associated with powerful and extraordinary acts beyond the range of human ability. John the Baptist refers to him as *'the Lamb of God'* and as *'a man who ranks ahead of me'*. The woman of Samaria found herself asking whether this really could be the Messiah. And although Pilate used the words, *'Here is the man!'* he knew that there was something extraordinary about this man who stood before him.

Peter also refers to Jesus as a man attested by God with deeds of power, wonders and signs. His humanness is emphasized, yet his divine nature is made known by God through wonders and signs. Similarly, Timothy states that Jesus fulfills his role as mediator between God and man in virtue of his being human. As a man he represents our humanness before God.

Jesus Christ Yesterday

The following passage comes from Mark's introduction to the account of the Feeding of the Five Thousand. Although no specific reference is made to the humanity of Jesus, Mark portrays the human quality of Jesus' response to the tiredness of the disciples and the needs of the crowd:

'The apostles gathered around Jesus, and told him all that they had done and taught. He said to them, "Come away to a deserted place all by yourselves and rest a while." For many were coming and going, and they had no leisure even to eat. And they went away in the boat to a deserted place by themselves. Now many saw them going and recognized them, and they hurried there on foot from all the towns and arrived ahead of them. As he went ashore, he saw a great crowd; and he had compassion on them, because they were like sheep without a shepherd; and he began to teach them many things,' (Mark 6: 30 -34).

DISCUSSION

1. What human qualities do you recognize in Jesus' attitude towards the disciples and the crowd in the above narrative? What significance do they have for our understanding of the person of Jesus?
2. What did Pilate mean when he said, 'Here is the man!'?
3. How does understanding the human nature of Jesus help us to recognize his divine nature?
4. The picture of Jesus at the beginning of this study is the work of the Canadian artist, Willis S. Wheatley[2]. How do you respond to his portrayal of Jesus? Do you find it helpful to understand his humanness?

CONCLUSION

The group leader should summarize the main points made in the discussion. The following passage from 'The Humility of God,' by John Macquarrie[3], should be read by a member of the group:

Jesus Christ Yesterday

"In the original experience of the disciples, they attached themselves to the wholly human person, Jesus of Nazareth. They certainly thought of him as a human being long before anyone believed that he was God incarnate. Even after their experiences of the risen Christ had persuaded them that the crucified one was now the Lord of life, they expressed this by saying that God had exalted the man Jesus to his Lordship. All this is important, and must not be forgotten, for otherwise it is easy to forget that Jesus was truly man and we come to think of him as an entirely supernatural being. But as the disciples thought further on the significance of Jesus Christ – and as we think more deeply on what it would mean for a man to manifest the nature of God – then it becomes clear that a human being could only be exalted to the side of God if God had already taken the initiative and descended into that human being."

Time of silence and free prayer to be concluded by saying together

    By the humanity of Jesus:
Lord, reveal yourself to us.
    By the prayers of Jesus:
Lord, teach us to pray.
    By the compassion of Jesus:
Lord, teach us to care for one another.
    By the labour of Jesus:
Lord, teach us how to work.
    By the love of Jesus:
Lord, teach us to love.
    By the cross of Jesus:
Lord, teach us to live. Amen.

Hymn: *'What grace, O Lord, and beauty shone,' (C.H. 216)*

THE BLESSING

Jesus Christ Yesterday

STUDY 2.

JESUS THE PROPHET

AIM
To examine the references in the gospels to Jesus as a prophet and rabbi, and to consider the importance of his Jewishness to our understanding of his teaching and person and to the relationship between Christianity and Judaism today.

WELCOME AND OPENING DEVOTIONS
Hymn: *'May the mind of Christ my Saviour,'* (C.H. 432) and opening prayer.

STARTING POINT
A first glance at newly developed photographs sets us blushing at embarrassing and unflattering pictures of ourselves, but we are pleased with those in which we look reasonably becoming! Although we are told that the camera never lies, we prefer photographs that depict us in a favourable light.

The gospels contain a series of pictures of Jesus, but as the Church wrestled with the deeper meaning of his person and work it tended to give greater prominence to some images rather than others. Among those neglected were references to Jesus as a prophet, a teacher and a rabbi. While the term *prophet* does not adequately convey the full significance of the life and person of Jesus, at the same time[2] the earliest accounts depict him as a Jewish rabbi and recent studies have emphasized the importance of the Jewish background to the gospels and their portrait of Jesus the Jew.

Two significant topics arise from the image of Jesus as prophet, namely the importance of his teaching, and the significance of his Jewish background to our understanding of his person and his work. In relation to his teaching, we see a careful balance between the demands of the Law and the ethics of the Kingdom: *'You have heard that it was said to those of ancient*

Jesus Christ Yesterday

times... But I say to you...' This was not to say that the teaching of the Kingdom was to replace the Law and the prophets, but rather to fulfil them (Matt. 5:17).

In interpreting the person of Jesus the gospel writers stated, on the one hand, that Jesus stood in succession to the great prophets of Israel, but on the other hand, he was also greater than a prophet and the one to whom all the previous prophets pointed and of whom they spoke. *'The law indeed was given through Moses, grace and truth came through Jesus Christ,'* (John 1:17). It is right to call Jesus a prophet, but equally it is wrong to regard him as *only* a prophet. The result is that in Christian teaching other titles, such as Christ and Lord have superceded *prophet* and *rabbi*, particularly as Christianity distanced itself from its Jewish roots, and later reacted against the Islamic belief in Jesus as a great prophet. Is it possible that the seeds of later hostility between Christianity, Judaism and Islam were sown when the gospel emphasis upon Jesus the prophet was forgotten? Is this not an emphasis that needs to be recovered today?

In this connection it is worth considering the words of the church historian, Jaroslav Pelikan, in his book, *Jesus Through the Centuries* [4]:

'The question is easier to ask than it is to answer, and it is easier to avoid than it is to ask in the first place. But ask it we must: Would there have been an Auschwitz, if every Christian church and every Christian home had focused its devotion on Mary not as Mother of God and Queen of Heaven but as the Jewish maiden and the new Miriam, and on icons of Christ not only as Pantocrator but as Rabbi Jeshua bar-Joseph, Rabbi Jesus of Nazareth, the Son of David, in the context of the history of a suffering Israel and a suffering humanity?'

Has Christian belief centred on Christ as Lord and saviour at the expense of Christ as prophet and teacher? Do you think that Jewish-Christian relations would have been more harmonious had Christianity given greater prominence to the Jewishness of Jesus?

Jesus Christ Yesterday

BIBLE STUDY

Jesus is described as a prophet by those who clearly saw his greatness, but who did not recognize him as the Son of God. The report brought to Herod was that Jesus was one of the old prophets who had risen from the dead:

'Now Herod the ruler heard about all that had taken place, and he was perplexed, because it was said by some that John had been raised from the dead, by some that Elijah had appeared, and by others that one of the ancient prophets had arisen. Herod said, "John I beheaded; but who is this about whom I hear such things?" And he tried to see him.' (Luke 9: 7-9).

Jesus asked what people were saying about him:

'Now when Jesus came into the district of Caesarea Philippi, he asked his disciples, "Who do people say the Son of Man is?" And they said, "Some say John the Baptist, but others Elijah, and still others Jeremiah or one of the prophets."' (Matthew 16: 13-14).

The verdict of the people during the Triumphal Entry was that Jesus was a prophet:

'"When he entered Jerusalem, the whole city was in turmoil, asking, "Who is this?" The crowds were saying, "This is the prophet Jesus from Nazareth in Galilee"' (Matthew 21: 10-11).

On more than one occasion Jesus used the word prophet to describe himself:

'And he said, "Truly I tell you, no prophet is accepted in the prophet's home town."' (Luke 4:24). '"Yet today, tomorrow, and the next day I must be on my way, because it is impossible for a prophet to be killed away from Jerusalem."' (Luke 13: 33).

The special status of Jesus as a prophet and teacher in the opinion of the people is declared at the end of the Sermon on the Mount:

'Now when Jesus had finished saying these things, the crowds were astonished at his teaching, for he taught them as one having authority, and not as their scribes.' (Matthew 7: 28-29).

From the passages selected we see that the title *prophet* as applied to

Jesus Christ Yesterday

Jesus contains a number of elements.

Firstly, the mighty acts of Jesus were associated with the conviction that he was a prophet. A prophet was understood to be a person in a close relationship to God, empowered by him to act supernaturally.

Secondly, Jesus was regarded as one sent from God. To connect him with Elijah and Jeremiah was to believe that he had been sent into the world by God. As no prophet had appeared for over three centuries, for Jesus to be seen as a prophet was highly significant.

Thirdly, his status as a prophet was confirmed by the way people marvelled at his teaching and recognized a special authority in his words.

Fourthly, the prophets were characteristically martyrs. The true prophet was the man who was always ready to lay down his life in the work of proclaiming the word of God. Jesus saw that to obey the will of God meant total obedience, even to the point of death.

DISCUSSION

1. The task of the prophet is not to foretell the future but to proclaim God's word in the present to his own age and generation. Do you agree? If so, is the word *prophet* a suitable description of Jesus?
2. Considering the decline in moral standards in society today, should more emphasis be placed on the Ten Commandments and on the moral teaching of Jesus as conveyed in the Sermon on the Mount?
3. In what sense did Jesus teach *as one with authority?* What was the nature of the authority of Jesus?
4. The painting above depicts Jesus crucified wearing a *tallith*, the shawl of a Jewish rabbi. Around the cross are arranged scenes of Jews being persecuted. The title of the painting by a modern artist, Marc Chagall, is *White Crucifixion* [5]. What do you believe to be the message of the painting for today?

Jesus Christ Yesterday

CONCLUSION

After a summary of the main points of the discussion, a member of the group should read the following imaginary conversation between Jesus and a Jewish scribe from 'The Gospel According to the Son,' by Norman Mailer [6]:

"I look," I told the scribe, "to gather my flock from all places, from wherever they have been scattered. So I do not despise those who are uncircumcised or those who are ignorant of the Book."

"Are you saying that you would give a light to the gentiles?" he asked.

"Yes," I said. "That would be for the salvation of all."

The scribe was silent; I think he was weary. He had studied the teachings of the great prophets, and they had dreamed of the hour when God would bring salvation to Israel. But it had not come to pass. Was the scribe wondering whether this Galilean and his peasants could know more about salvation than our heroes and prophets, even the kings of the glorious and holy past?

I continued to speak. "The Lord," I said, "has made my mouth a sharp sword. In the shadow of his hand he has hidden me. He has told me: 'Raise up the tribes of Jacob and the strong reserve of Israel.' But he also said: 'I will give you a light to the gentiles in order that you may be my salvation unto all the ends of the earth.'"

To which the scribe said, "Is that not blasphemy?"

I replied, "It is what my Father has said."

On these words he left.

A time of silence and prayer to end with reading the following together

> Lord Jesus Christ,
> be our beginning, and be our end;
> be our way, and be our light;
> be our strength, and be our rest;
> be our Teacher, and be our truth;
> be our Prophet, and be our Head;
> be our life, our Lord, our all. Amen

Hymn: 'Lord, thy word abideth,' (C.H. 130).

THE BLESSING.

Jesus Christ Yesterday

STUDY 3.

JESUS THE HEALER

AIM
To examine the portrayal of Jesus in the gospels as a healer and to consider the place of healing in Christian life and experience today.

WELCOME AND OPENING DEVOTIONS
Hymn: *'Thine arm, O Lord, in days of old,' (C.H. 214) and opening prayer.*

STARTING POINT
The opening hymn by Edward Plumptre refers to the three aspects of the healing ministry of Jesus – the historical, contemporary spiritual healing, and healing through modern medical science. *'In days of old,'* the blind, the dumb, the lame and the leprous went to him for healing. As *'his touch brought life and health'* to the sick and needy of his own day, he is near to bless and heal those who come to him today. And he continues to work through those whose hands and eyes minister to the sick and suffering. The Christian healing ministry today is grounded in the relation between the historical example of Jesus, the contemporary spiritual ministry of the church, and the contribution and development of modern medicine. But we begin with the historical and try to understand how the first followers of Jesus understood his ministry of healing.

Healing and *health* are closely linked to the biblical understanding of salvation. In the Old Testament the original meaning of salvation is *liberation* – being set free from everything which restricts, limits and enslaves, such as the fear of enemies, sin, temptation, guilt, evil spirits, fear, hunger, oppression, sickness and death. Closely allied with the ideal of salvation as liberation is the emphasis upon *wholeness* and *fullness of life*.

Jesus Christ Yesterday

A word which brings together the concepts of salvation/liberation/wholeness/healing is *shalôm*, usually translated *peace*. But *shalôm* also means harmony and the restoration of the wholeness of life through the healing of the totality of human relationships – a right relationship 'upwards' to God, 'downwards' to the earth and the environment, 'outwards' towards our fellow men and women, and 'inwards' towards ourselves. When Jews use the word *shalôm* as a greeting to others they wish them the peace and blessedness that flow from wholeness, harmony and healing.

But healing/salvation/wholeness are not achieved through human knowledge and ingenuity, but through the work of God. This leads us to the central message of the New Testament, namely that it is in the life, ministry, death and resurrection of Jesus Christ that the power of God is seen at work restoring our relationship to him and making good all other relationships damaged by sin. In Jesus God came to reconcile us to himself, to our fellow human beings, to our circumstances and to ourselves. The healing miracles of Jesus are seen as signs of the approach of the kingdom of God and of the subjugation of the powers of evil. He not only healed people of physical illnesses, he also healed their minds and their souls and led them to life in all its fullness.

Bishop Morris Maddocks, in his book *The Christian Healing Ministry* [7], says this:

'A portrait of Jesus that does not contain a substantial element of healing is a false one... Constantly Jesus was surrounded by crowds who sought him out and invariably he healed their sick. The fact that Jesus healed, and healed so consistently, ministering to the total personality and to all who were brought to him, has too frequently been disregarded in the history and theology of the Church, and yet the evidence of the New Testament is there for all to see.'

What accounts for our neglect today of Jesus the healer?

Jesus Christ Yesterday

BIBLE STUDY

Healing figures prominently in the ministry of Jesus from the beginning and is seen as part of his appeal to the crowds:

'That evening, at sundown, they brought to him all who were sick or possessed with demons. And the whole city was gathered around the door. And he cured many who were sick with various diseases, and cast out many demons; and he would not permit the demons to speak, because they knew him' (Mark 1: 32-34).

On one occasion Jesus was accused of using demonic power to cast out demons, but he replied that his miracles were signs of the approach of the kingdom:

'If it is by the finger of God that I cast out the demons, then the kingdom of God has come to you' (Luke 11:20).

When the messengers of John the Baptist came to ask Jesus if he was the one who was to come, he answered by referring them to his miracles of healing:

'When the men had come to him, they said, "John the Baptist has sent us to you to ask, 'Are you the one who is to come, or are we to wait for another?'" Jesus had just then cured many people of diseases, plagues, and evil spirits, and had given sight to many who were blind. And he answered them, "Go and tell John what you have seen and heard: the blind receive their sight, the lame walk, the lepers are cleansed, the deaf hear, the dead are raised, the poor have good news brought to them. And blessed is anyone who takes no offence at me"'(Luke 7:20-23).

The miracles were proof of the saving power of God at work in the person of Jesus, and their purpose was primarily to give glory to God:

'Great crowds came to him, bringing with them the lame, the maimed, the blind, the mute, and many others. They put them at his feet, and he cured them, so that the crowd was amazed when they saw the mute speaking, the maimed whole, the lame walking, and the blind seeing. And

Jesus Christ Yesterday

they praised the God of Israel' (Matthew 15: 30-31).

His healing ministry is an inseparable part of the witness of the Gospels to the life and work of Jesus. One thing is plain, we cannot discover the 'real Jesus' by ignoring or putting aside his miracles of healing. But the main emphasis of the miracle stories is not on the power and authority of Jesus, for he did not perform miracles to draw attention to himself, but rather to bring glory to God.

The miracles of healing represent some fundamental truths about God, Jesus, the kingdom of God, and the realization of the promises of God through the prophets:

- The miracles are evidence of the compassion of God towards all who suffer and show clearly that sickness and suffering are in no way God's will nor are they sent as punishment from God.
- One of the main purposes of the miracles of healing was to help people to see the saving power of God at work in the person of Jesus.
- For Jesus himself his healing ministry signified that the kingdom of God had come near. Although the kingdom is yet to come in its fullness, its nearness and its power are to be seen in the person and work of Jesus.
- In the miracles one of the central promises of the Old Testament is fulfilled, namely that God will heal his people physically and spiritually in the time of their salvation (See Isaiah 35: 3-6).

Jesus Christ Yesterday

DISCUSSION

1. Do you agree that the miracles of healing demonstrate clearly that sickness and suffering are contrary to God's will and purpose for humanity?
2. In what ways does the portrayal of Jesus as a healer contribute to our understanding of his person and his work?
3. 'Because it is the purpose of God that people should attain to wholeness of body, mind and spirit, healing is a central element in the biblical understanding of salvation.'
   Discuss.
4. The sculpture shown above is entitled *Gesu medico* and is the work of Giovanni Meloni[8], a modern Italian sculptor. What does it convey about the need of the sick man, about Jesus' attitude towards him, and his manner of healing him?

Jesus Christ Yesterday

CONCLUSION

The main points of the discussion should be summarized. In preparation for the final prayers the following from 'The Forgotten Talent' by J. Cameron Peddie [9] should be read by a member of the group:

> 'The first and last word, I know, regarding divine healing rests of course with our Lord. We read that when he still was in the flesh he gave his disciples power to heal all manner of sickness and all manner of disease and was able to impart the necessary power directly to them. In a final interview with his friends before his ascension, he said, "You shall receive power, after that the Holy Spirit is come upon you, and you shall be witnesses to me." These words imply that the power is to be imparted through the Holy Spirit, but quite clearly is not to be identified with that spirit... Now it is with the powers of the kingdom that we are dealing in this healing ministry... The kingdom of heaven has as great a variety of divine energy as this material universe has, and these forms of divine power have been made available by the Creator to meet the needs of the children of men. They are mediated through Jesus Christ and the Holy Spirit has a part to play."

Jesus Christ Yesterday

A time of prayer, remembering particularly members of the church and of the community who are sick. The following prayer to be said together:

> *Lord Jesus Christ, our healer and saviour,*
> *hear our prayer for those in sickness and in pain,*
> *and those who are anxious and troubled in spirit:*
> *reach out to them in your power*
> *to ease their pain of body and distress of mind,*
> *to lighten their darkness,*
> *and to bring them life, hope and healing,*
> *for your name's sake. Amen.*

Hymn: *"How sweet the name of Jesus sounds'* (C.H. 376).

THE BLESSING

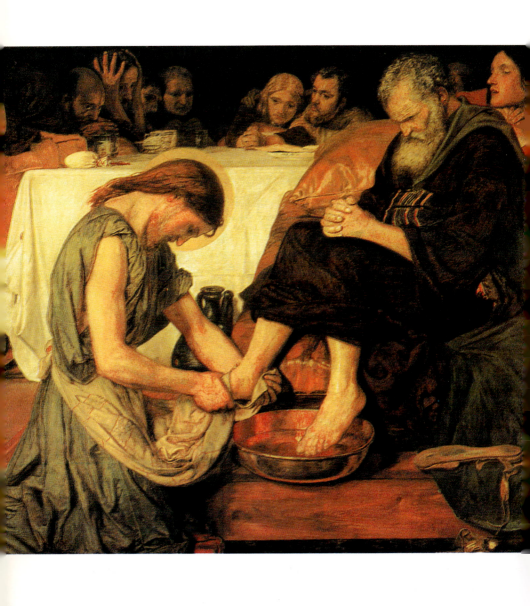

Jesus Christ Yesterday

STUDY 4
JESUS THE SERVANT

AIM
To examine the extent to which Jesus interpreted his ministry in terms of the Suffering Servant of Isaiah, and to consider the importance of service in the Christian life.

WELCOME AND OPENING DEVOTIONS
Hymn: *'O Master, let me walk with thee'* (C.H. 436) and brief opening prayer.

STARTING POINT
The word most often used for *servant* in the New Testament can also be translated *slave*. In the days of Jesus servants did not enjoy any kind of status or rights. They were expected to do the most menial of tasks and to obey their master's commands without question. At the same time, for Jews, the title *servant* had important historical and religious associations. The phrase *Servant of God* was a proud title given to any man who was considered to have dedicated himself to serve the purpose of God. Abraham, Moses, Caleb, Joshua, Elijah and Isaiah are all referred to as God's servants.

Among the prophetic writings of the Second Isaiah (Isaiah 40-58) we find a number of passages known as *The Servant Songs*. No one can be certain of the identity of this particular servant, sometimes he seems to represent Israel, sometimes a specific group of people within Israel, sometimes one of the heroes of the faith, and sometimes a future messianic leader. It is clear that Jesus was familiar with the Servant Songs of Isaiah, and even more clear that the writers of the gospels believed that Jesus, in his life, and particularly in his suffering and death, fulfilled the ideals of the Servant.

Jesus Christ Yesterday

As the way of the Suffering Servant led to sacrifice, suffering and death, Jesus must have been aware that the experience of the Servant as described in Isaiah 53 corresponded to the humiliation and sacrifice he would be called upon to suffer if people were to reject him and to scorn his message. But that is not to say that Jesus consciously adopted the mission of the Servant of the Lord, or that he regarded himself as fulfilling the Old Testament prophecies, even though the early Christians regarded him in those terms.

Nowhere does Jesus himself claim to be the servant in the privileged and official sense of the Jewish messianic tradition. Rather, he spoke of himself as *the servant of all*, and emphasized the importance of lowliness and service in people's relationships to each other and to God. The story which best illustrates Jesus' ministry of service is the account of his washing his disciples' feet. This is how William Temple explains the significance of this event in his *Readings in St. John's Gospel* [10]:

'We rather shrink from this revelation. We are ready, perhaps, to be humble before God; but we do not want him to be humble in his dealings with us. We should like him, who has the right, to glory in his goodness and greatness; then we, as we pass from his presence, may be entitled to pride ourselves on such achievements as distinguish us above other men. But the worship of Jesus makes that impossible to justify... The divine humility shews itself in rendering service. He who is entitled to claim the service of all his creatures chooses first to give his service to them... Every disciple and every company of disciples need to learn that their first duty is to let Christ serve them. For them the first duty is to let the Lord cleanse them by his word in their whole persons, and still to let him cleanse them day by day from stains that come from life in the world; and at all times to leave the Lord to do with them as he will.'

Why are we reluctant to allow Jesus to serve us?

Jesus Christ Yesterday

BIBLE STUDY

When Jesus withdrew in the face of the opposition of the Pharisees, Matthew saw this as a fulfilment of the prophecy of Isaiah:

'Many crowds followed him, and he cured them all, and he ordered them not to make him known. This was to fulfil what had been spoken through the prophet Isaiah:

"Here is my servant, whom I have chosen,
my beloved, with whom my soul is well pleased.
I have put my spirit upon him,
and he will proclaim justice to the Gentiles.
He will not wrangle or cry aloud,
nor will anyone hear his voice in the streets.
He will not break a bruised reed
or quench a smouldering wick
until he brings justice to victory.
And in his name the Gentiles will hope"' (Matthew 12: 15-21).

Following the request of the mother of James and John that her sons be given places of honour in the kingdom, Jesus had this to say to his disciples:

'Jesus called them to him and said, "You know that the rulers of the Gentiles lord it over them, and their great ones are tyrants over them. It will not be so among you; but whoever wishes to be great among you must be your servant, and whoever wishes to be first among you must be your slave; just as the Son of Man came not to be served, but to serve, and to give his life a ransom for many"' (Matthew 20: 25-28).

Jesus Christ Yesterday

In another version of the same story told by Luke, Jesus says:

> The greatest among you must become like the youngest, and the leader like one who serves. For who is greater, the one who sits at the table or the one who serves? Is it not the one at the table? But I am among you as one who serves' (Luke 22:26-27).

After Jesus had washed his disciples' feet he gave them instructions to follow his example and serve one another:

'After he had washed their feet, and put on his robe, and had returned to the table, he said to them, "Do you know what I have done to you? You call me Teacher and Lord – and you are right, for that is what I am. So if I, your Lord and Teacher, have washed your feet, you also ought to wash one another's feet. For I have set you an example, that you also should do as I have done to you"' (John 13: 12-15).

The gospel writers, especially Matthew, believed that Jesus fulfilled Isaiah's prophecies about the Suffering Servant, especially in his humility and his willingness to suffer and to sacrifice himself for the sake of others. At the same time, Jesus understood his ministry in terms of a more basic and common form of service which involved giving himself in compassion and service to God and to his fellows. According to Jesus the servant

– the essence of love is service;
– the condition of service is humility;
– the consequence of humility is the discovery of true greatness.

Jesus Christ Yesterday

DISCUSSION

1. What is the meaning and what are the conditions of service according to the teaching and example of Jesus?
2. How should the church today continue the ministry of Jesus the Servant? Think of specific projects and forms of service your church could undertake in the community.
3. Are we more inclined to seek authority and dignity in terms of worldly importance and recognition rather than in terms of service and humility?
4. The picture accompanying this study of Jesus washing the feet of his disciples is the work of Ford Madox Brown[11]. Brown emulated the naturalistic style of the Italian Pre-Raphaelites, and in this painting he portrays Jesus as an ordinary serving man performing the menial task of a slave. Does his portrayal of Jesus help us to understand the dignity of service? What, in your view, is the reaction of Peter and the other disciples?

Jesus Christ Yesterday

CONCLUSION

Draw the discussion to a close and ask members of the group to share their ideas of specific forms of service the church could undertake. A member of the group to read 'The Servant Song' by Richard Gillard [12]:

> *Brother, let me be your servant,*
> *let me be as Christ to you;*
> *pray that I may have the grace*
> *to let you be my servant too.*
>
> *We are pilgrims on a journey,*
> *and companions on the road;*
> *we are here to help each other*
> *walk the mile and bear the load.*
>
> *I will hold the Christ-light for you*
> *in the night-time of your fear;*
> *I will hold my hand out to you,*
> *speak the peace you long to hear.*
>
> *I will weep when you are weeping;*
> *when you laugh I'll laugh with you.*
> *I will share your joy and sorrow*
> *till we've seen this journey through.*
>
> *When we sing to God in heaven*
> *we shall find such harmony,*
> *born of all we've known together*
> *of Christ's love and agony.*

Jesus Christ Yesterday

Sister, let me be your servant,
let me be as Christ to you;
pray that I may have the grace
to let you be my servant too.

A time of prayer and reflection, to conclude with reading together:

Lord Jesus Christ,
you came among us in humility,
taking upon yourself our human nature;
help us to follow your holy example
and to be ready always to offer to those in need
our compassion, our companionship and our help.
Show us the glory that is found in humility
and the dignity that is found in obedience;
for your name's sake. Amen.

Hymn: *'Forth in thy Name, O Lord, I go'* (C. H. 463)

THE BLESSING

Jesus Christ Today

STUDY 5.

JESUS SON OF GOD

AIM
To consider how the contemporaries of Jesus came to believe in a divine aspect to his character and to discuss whether the term 'Son of God' is the most appropriate title to describe his divinity today.

WELCOME AND OPENING DEVOTIONS
Hymn: *'God and Father, we adore thee'* (C.H.369) and prayer.

STARTING POINT
In the four studies which follow we shall be looking at the significance of Jesus for today.

Central to Jewish faith was the belief that there is but one God, and Jesus, like all Jews of his day, shared this conviction. Throughout their history the Jews had defended their religion against the influence of neighbouring pagan cults that worshipped many gods. And yet, within a generation after the crucifixion the followers of Jesus were confessing him to be the *'Son of God'* and were speaking of him in terms which previously they would only have used to speak of God himself. They prayed to Jesus, they worshipped him, and they claimed him to be the long-expected Messiah and the full and final revelation of the nature of God.

How did such a development take place? Did Jesus himself claim to be the Son of God, or did his followers adopt the term to express their conviction that Jesus was more than an ordinary human being and that his character and ministry bore the marks of divinity? There is little evidence in the gospels that Jesus attributed the title directly to himself. At the same time, it is clear that Jesus was aware of a close personal relationship between

Jesus Christ Today

himself and God, similar to a relationship between a gracious father and a loving son. Although it is impossible for us to penetrate the deepest personal experiences of Jesus, we can see that throughout his life he was conscious of a deep mystical communion with God out of which sprang his moral strength, his compassion towards all in need and the power of his personality and influence. The expression 'my Father' was often on his lips and the extraordinary impact of his character and example cannot be explained apart from his union with his heavenly Father and his total dependence upon him.

His followers became increasingly aware that in the company of Jesus they were with one who could not be adequately described only in human categories. The conviction grew within them that when they were with Jesus they were in the presence of God. He spoke with divine authority. He performed healing miracles which he attributed to the power of God at work in him. His greatness became most clearly evident in his humility, his tenderness and his total self-denial. Increasingly his disciples knew that God himself was meeting them in the life and person of Jesus and in an attempt to put their conviction into words they adopted terms like 'Messiah', 'Lord,' 'The Word,' and 'Son of God' to describe him.

Christian experience and faith over the centuries have confirmed the witness of the New Testament. People today as in the past encounter Jesus, not as a historical figure belonging to an age long past, but as a living person – one who shows us what God is like and one who can transform our lives and the life of the world. The transforming impact of Jesus is the theme of the well-known and anonymous words, *'One Solitary Life.'*

> *He was born in an obscure village*
> *He worked in a carpenter's shop until he was thirty.*
> *Then for three years he became an itinerant preacher.*
> *He never held an office.*

Jesus Christ Today

He never had a family or owned a house.
He didn't go to college.
He never wrote a book.
He had no credentials but himself...

Twenty centuries have come and gone,
and today he is the central figure of the human race.
All the armies that ever marched,
and all the parliaments that ever sat,
and all the kings that ever reigned,
have not affected the life of man
on this earth as much as that
   ONE SOLITARY LIFE.*

Can the impact of this 'One Solitary Life' be explained without the claim that God was at work in him?

BIBLE STUDY

It was after Jesus' awareness of his divine sonship was confirmed in his baptism that he set out on his public ministry:

"In those days Jesus came from Nazareth of Galilee and was baptized by John in the river Jordan. And just as he was coming up out of the water, he saw the heavens torn apart and the Spirit descending like a dove on him. And a voice came from heaven, "You are my son, the Beloved, with you I am well pleased." (Mark 1: 9 – 11).

In the wilderness the tempter tried to raise doubts in Jesus' mind about his divine sonship:

'He fasted for forty days and forty nights, and afterwards he was famished. The tempter came and said to him, "If you are the Son of God, command these stones to become loaves of bread..." Then the devil took

Jesus Christ Today

him to the holy city and placed him on the pinnacle of the temple, saying to him, "If you are the Son of God, throw yourself down..."' (Matthew 4: 2 – 3 ; 5 – 6).

On more than one occasion in the gospels we find a close connection between the terms 'Messiah' and 'Son of God', as in the confession of Peter at Caesarea Philippi:

'Now when Jesus came into the district of Caesarea Philippi, he asked his disciples, "Who do people say that the Son of Man is?" And they said, "Some say John the Baptist, but others Elijah, and still others Jeremiah or one of the prophets." He said to them, "But who do you say that I am?" Simon Peter answered, "You are the Messiah, the Son of the living God." And Jesus answered him, "Blessed are you, Simon son of Jonah! For flesh and blood has not revealed this to you, but my Father in heaven"' (Matthew 16:13 – 17)

Jesus is regularly described as 'the Son' in John's Gospel, particularly in the references to his close and mystical relationship to his Father:

'Jesus said to them, "Very truly, I tell you, the Son can do nothing on his own, but only what he sees the Father doing: for whatever the Father does, the Son does likewise. The Father loves the Son and shows him all that he himself is doing; and he will show him greater works than these, so that you will be astonished"' (John 5: 19 – 20).

The main ideas in these passages of Scripture can be summed up in this way:
- the awareness of being the Son of God developed gradually in the mind of Jesus and it was following the confirmation of his sonship in his baptism that he began his public ministry;
- although doubts arose in his mind during his temptation in the wilderness, Jesus never lost his sense of divine sonship, which was the source of his influence and moral power;
- Jesus knew that he could not coerce people into believing in him as

Jesus Christ Today

    Messiah and Son of God and that everyone would have to discover him for themselves;

–   it is in his deep personal relationship with God and his emphasis upon God as Father that we grasp the true significance of the term 'Son of God' as a description of Jesus.

DISCUSSION

1. Would you agree that Jesus cannot be fully and properly defined in human terms alone, for example, as a good man, a powerful prophet or a religious genius?
2. Which elements in the person and work of Jesus impress upon you his divine nature?
3. Does the term 'Son of God' adequately convey to our age the Christian belief in Jesus as truly man and truly God?
4. For his portrayal of Jesus (c.1610)[13], El Greco took as a model a young Jewish man from Toledo. His intention was to depict the divinity of Jesus reflected through his humanness. It has been said that in this painting El Greco succeeded in creating a synthesis of the commonplace, the artistic and the mystical. Do you agree?

Jesus Christ Today

CONCLUSION

Following a summing up of the discussion the following concluding passage from Albert Schweitzer's 'The Quest of the Historical Jesus' [14] *should be read by a member of the group:*

> *'The ways in which men expressed their recognition of him, such as Messiah, Son of Man, Son of God, have become for us historical parables. We can find no designation which expresses what he is for us. He comes to us as one unknown, without a name, as of old, by the lake-side, he came to those who knew him not. He speaks to us the same word, "Follow thou me!" and sets us to the tasks which he has to fulfil for our time. He commands. And to those who obey him, whether they be wise or simple, he will reveal himself in the toils, the conflicts, the sufferings which they shall pass through in his fellowship, and, as an ineffable mystery, they shall learn in their own experience who he is.'*

Jesus Christ Today

Time for silence and prayer to be concluded by saying together

> *Lord Jesus Christ, Son of God,*
> *our saviour and our friend,*
> *we thank you for your unfailing mercy*
> *and for your infinite love*
> *freeing us from our sins*
> *and reconciling us to God;*
> *send us out in the power of your Spirit*
> *to live and work to your praise and glory. Amen.*

Hymn: *'O Jesus, I have promised'* (C.H. 434)

THE BLESSING.

Jesus Christ Today

STUDY 6

JESUS THE SAVIOUR

AIM
To look at the New Testament interpretation of salvation and of God's saving work in Jesus Christ, and to consider in what sense Jesus is saviour in our experience today?

WELCOME AND OPENING DEVOTIONS
Hymn: *'God is my strong salvation'* (C.H. 404) and a brief opening prayer.

STARTING POINT
Of all the titles used within Christian literature and devotion to describe Jesus none is more dear and precious than the title *saviour*. Although the title is seldom used directly to speak of Jesus in the gospels, of the fact that the early Christians experienced him as their saviour, through whom they had been reconciled to God, there can be no doubt.

In the Old Testament we find the word saviour applied almost exclusively to God. Isaiah prays to *'the God of Israel, the saviour'* (Is. 45: 12, 21), while the Psalms frequently refer to *'God, my saviour'* or *'God, our salvation'* (e.g. Psalms 24: 5; 27:9; 65:5; 79:9). Similarly there are numerous occasions in the New Testament when God is described as saviour. In the Song of Mary we hear, *'My spirit rejoices in God my Saviour'* (Luke 1:47). Paul is an apostle *'by the command of God, our saviour'* (1 Tim. 1:1). Salvation is seen as the action of God, and so it follows that it is God who is at work in Jesus Christ reconciling people to himself. This must always be kept in the forefront of our thinking as it rules out any notion that Jesus came to persuade a reluctant and vindictive God to look favourably on human kind. Jesus did not come to change the attitude of God towards

Jesus Christ Today

man, but to change the attitude of man towards God.

The word translated as *salvation* or *redemption* has more than one shade of meaning. It can mean *being set free from danger, oppression or captivity*, and includes the notion of *the healing of disease and being released from death*. Salvation can also include the image of *being set free from evil and temptation* and all that would separate man from God. This wide range of meanings can be found in the gospels especially with regard to the work and impact of Jesus. Jesus came to save the whole person – body mind and spirit, our relationships with other people, with the world around us, with ourselves and with God. The New Testament makes it clear that the experience of salvation is the heart of the Christian life, an experience gained through knowing Jesus and through faith in him.

This is no abstract biblical concept, but an experience shared by Christians over the centuries. Jesus is our saviour today precisely because people still experience the reality of release from sin, reconciliation to God and to one another, and the joy of discovering new meaning and purpose to their lives through trust in the saving love of God made known to him.

This was the experience, which came to him at the Communion Table in Talgarth Church on Whitsunday 1735, which changed the life of Howel Harris, Trefeca.

In his diary for that eventful day these words appear [15]:

'At the Table, the sight of Christ bleeding upon the cross was kept continually before my eyes and I was helped to believe that I was receiving forgiveness through the merit of that blood. I was relieved of my burden. I returned home leaping with joy. On the way I said to a neighbour who looked sad, "Why the sadness? I know my sins are forgiven!" O blessed day! O that I could but remember it with gratitude for ever!"'

What do you think Howel Harris meant when he spoke of holding the sight of Christ bleeding on the cross continually before his eyes? Is it only through

Jesus Christ Today

an encounter similar to that of Harris that the experience of salvation can become real to us today?

BIBLE STUDY

According to the First Letter of John, it was as a consequence of their experience of seeing Jesus and of bearing witness to him that the first believers came to recognize him and to confess him as saviour:

'And we have seen and do testify that the Father has sent his Son as the Saviour of the world. God abides in those who confess that Jesus is the Son of God, and they abide in God. So we have known and believe the love that God has for us' (1 John 4: 14-16).

In the gospels Jesus says that those who deny themselves, take up the cross and follow him will save their lives:

'Then Jesus told his disciples, "If any want to become my followers, let them deny themselves and take up their cross and follow me. For those who want to save their life will lose it, and those who lose their life for my sake will find it. For what will it profit them if they gain the whole world but forfeit their life? Or what will they give in return for their life?"' (Matthew 16: 24-26).

Following the account of the meeting between Jesus and Nicodemus, John's Gospel tells us that God sent his Son, not to condemn the world, but to show his love for the world:

'For God so loved the world that he gave his only Son, so that everyone who believes in him may not perish but may have eternal life. Indeed, God did not send the Son into the world to condemn the world, but in order that the world might be saved through him' (John 3: 16-17).

In speaking of himself in John's Gospel as the door to the sheepfold and as the good shepherd, Jesus says that he has come to save his people and to lead them to abundant life:

'"I am the gate. Whoever enters by me will be saved, and will come

Jesus Christ Today

in and go out and find pasture. The thief comes only to steal and kill and destroy. I came that they might have life, and have it abundantly. I am the good shepherd. The good shepherd lays down his life for the sheep'" (John 10: 9-11).

As salvation through Christ is entirely the work of God, there is nothing we can do to gain or to merit salvation. We are saved only through the gracious action of God:

'God, who is rich in mercy, out of the great love with which he loved us even when we were dead through our trespasses, made us alive together with Christ – by grace you have been saved – and raised us up with him and seated us with him in the heavenly places in Christ Jesus, so that in the ages to come he might show the immeasurable riches of his grace in kindness towards us in Christ Jesus. For by grace you have been saved through faith, and this is not your own doing; it is the gift of God – not the result of works, so that no one may boast. For we are what he has made us, created in Christ Jesus for good works, which God prepared beforehand to be our way of life' (Ephesians 2: 4-10).

Man's deepest need is the restoration of his relationship to God, to his fellow men and women and to his circumstances and to the world around him, a relationship which has been broken by his rebellion against God, disobedience to the laws of God, and a self-centredness indifferent to other people and their needs. That is essentially what the Bible calls sin. The above passages impress upon us

- that God is at work reconciling us to himself and to one another;
- that God's reconciling love has been revealed and activated in the life and death of Jesus Christ;
- that the condition of reconciliation and new life are to deny the self, to trust in Jesus and to follow him;
- that the consequence of salvation is an experience of liberation and fulfilment.

Jesus Christ Today

DISCUSSION

1. The word salvation can also be translated as *liberation, healing, reconciliation* or *wholeness*. Which term best conveys the meaning of salvation for today?
2. Would you agree that the restoration of our relationships to one another, to ourselves and to our circumstances, depends upon the restoration of our relationship to God?
3. If the purpose of God in sending Jesus was to make known his love for the world, what do we learn of the nature of God's love from the life, death and resurrection of Jesus?
4. The sculpture entitled *The Tortured Christ* (1975)[16] pictured above is the work of the Brazilian artist, Guido Rocha. Rocha, who was himself tortured in a Brazilian prison, depicts Jesus identifying himself with all the suffering people of the world, especially those who suffer torture and persecution. Does his work help us to understand the significance for today of Jesus' saving action on the cross?

Jesus Christ Today

CONCLUSION

After a summing up of the discussion a member of the group should read Sheila Cassidy's 'Credo'[17]:

> I believe that God
> has the whole world in his hands.
> He is not a bystander
> at the pain of the world.
>
> He does not stand like Peter
> wringing his hands in the shadows
> but is there, in the dock, on the rack,
> high on the gallows tree.
> He is in the pain of the lunatic, the tortured,
> those racked by grief.
> His is the blood that flows in the gutter,
> His are the veins burned by heroin,
> His the lungs choked by AIDS.
> His is the heart broken by suffering,
> His the despair
> of the mute, the oppressed,
> the man with a gun to his head.
>
> He is the God of Paradox,
> the God of Power made impotent,
> the God of Love.

Jesus Christ Today

A time for silence and free prayer to be concluded with saying together

> *We praise you, O Lord,*
> *that through Jesus Christ*
> *you have reconciled us to yourself.*
> *Help us to know him, to love him,*
> *and to share with others the good news of your love,*
> *that they too may find newness of life*
> *in him who died and rose again for our salvation:*
> *your Son and our Saviour, Jesus Christ. Amen.*

Hymn: 'And can it be, that I should gain' (C.H. 409).

THE BENEDICTION.

Jesus Christ Today

STUDY 7

JESUS, THE LORD

AIM

To discover how the early Christians came to think of Jesus primarily as Lord and to discuss what it means to confess the lordship of Jesus Christ today.

WELCOME AND OPENING DEVOTIONS
Hymn: *'Jesus, Lord, Redeemer'* (C.H. 283) followed by a brief prayer.

STARTING POINT
It is thought that the very earliest Christian confession was *'Jesus is Lord!'* In an early Christian document known as the *Didache*, probably written towards the end of the first century, the following directions are given with regard to the celebration of the Lord's Supper: *'On the Lord's Day, after all have assembled, break bread and give thanks, after you have first confessed your transgressions... Do not permit any to eat or drink of your Eucharist but those who have been baptized in the Lord's name.'* The early believers not only referred to Jesus as Lord, but went so far as to describe the first day of the week on which they met to worship as *'the Lord's Day'*.

In the days of Jesus the title Lord had a familial, social and political, as well as religious significance. The word was used to describe the head of the family, a slave master, an employer, or any person in authority, not as a title but as a term of courtesy, just as we might greet someone as 'Sir'. Only in the case of kings and emperors was *Lord* used as an official title. But the word also had religious connotations, especially for Jews, for whom God was the only true Lord.

It is not difficult to understand how Gentile Christians came to address Jesus as *Lord*, but it is more difficult to understand how Christians

Jesus Christ Today

of a Jewish background, who thought of God alone as Lord, came to do so. What at first gained only gradual acceptance became, after the resurrection, the inevitable and most commonly adopted title for Jesus. There could be no other explanation for the extraordinary phenomenon of this man who had lived, died and risen from the dead, than to say that he was the Lord of life and death and shared in the very lordship of God himself.

It was precisely the confession that 'Jesus Christ is Lord' that brought the early church into head-on collision with the Roman Empire. This was the confession for which Christians were martyred and for which they were prepared to die. In an attempt to unify the empire the Roman government made Caesar worship compulsory. Once a year citizens were required to burn a pinch of incense to acknowledge the divinity of the Emperor and to say, 'Caesar is Lord!' This was what Christians could never do. They refused to attribute the title *Lord* in a religious sense to anyone but to Jesus, and so they chose to die rather than compromise their faith.

The choice between obeying or denying the lordship of Christ is one that faces Christians today as in every age. One who was faced with this choice and who suffered martyrdom for his uncompromising stand against oppression and tyranny was Archbishop Oscar Romero, of San Salvador. It was while he was delivering a homily, of which the following words are an extract[18], that he was shot in March 1980:

'The hope of a new earth should not weaken, but reinvigorate our concern to perfect this earth where the body of the new human family is already growing, a body which can be a foreshadowing of the new age. So, although we have to make a careful distinction between temporal progress and the growth of Christ's kingdom, temporal progress, insofar as it may contribute to a better ordering of human society, is still of great importance to the kingdom of God for Christ is Lord of all the earth.

When we have spread human dignity, unity and freedom throughout the earth in the spirit of the Lord and in accordance with his command, we

Jesus Christ Today

will find that when Christ surrenders the eternal and universal kingdom to the Father, these fruits will be free of all stain, illuminated and transformed. His kingdom will be a kingdom of truth and life, a kingdom of holiness and grace, a kingdom of justice, love and peace. Where Christ rules as Lord in the hearts of his people the kingdom is already mysteriously present on our earth. When the Lord comes again its perfection will be completed.'

What other powers seek to gain lordship over our lives today? Are we in danger of being drawn unaware under their authority?

BIBLE STUDY

In the gospels the word Lord is used to emphasize the importance of obeying Jesus and submitting to the will of God:

'Not everyone who says to me, "Lord, Lord" will enter the kingdom of heaven, but only one who does the will of my Father in heaven. On that day many will say to me, "Lord, Lord, did we not prophesy in your name, and cast out demons in your name, and do many deeds of power in your name?" Then I will declare to them, "I never knew you; go away from me you evildoers"' (Matthew 7: 21-23).

The title *Lord* applied to Jesus only has its full meaning after the resurrection, for example, in Thomas' confession after his encounter with the risen Jesus in the upper room:

'A week later his disciples were again in the house, and Thomas was with them. Although the doors were shut, Jesus came and stood among them and said, "Peace be with you." Then he said to Thomas, "Put your finger here and see my hands. Reach out your hand and put it in my side. Do not doubt but believe." Thomas answered him, "My Lord and my God!" Jesus said to him, "Have you believed because you have seen me? Blessed are those who have not seen and yet come to believe"' (John 20: 26-29).

Jesus Christ Today

Paul claims that to confess Jesus as Lord is the beginning of the Christian life and a condition of salvation:

'If you confess with your lips that Jesus is Lord and believe in your heart that God raised him from the dead, you will be saved. For one believes with the heart and so is justified and one confesses with the mouth and so is saved... For, "Everyone who calls on the name of the Lord shall be saved"' (Romans 10: 9-10, 13).

The lordship of Jesus is of a radically different order to that of temporal power and authority. Jesus is exalted by God and his name is praised and his lordship confessed by every tongue, because of his humility and self-emptying.

'Being found in human form, he humbled himself and became obedient to the point of death – even death on a cross. Therefore God also highly exalted him and gave him the name that is above every name, so that at the name of Jesus every knee should bend, in heaven and on earth and under the earth, and every tongue should confess that Jesus Christ is Lord, to the glory of God the Father' (Philippians 2: 8-11).

The themes contained in these passages point us to the reasons why the early church recognized and confessed Jesus as Lord:

– because he shares in the nature and power of God;
– because to confess Jesus as Lord is a condition of receiving new life;
– because he claimed practical obedience from his disciples;
– because, unlike temporal authorities, the glory and authority of Jesus as Lord are to be seen in his humility and simplicity;
– because he is seen as the object of the praise and worship of the church in heaven.

Jesus Christ Today

DISCUSSION

1. Can we believe in the lordship of Jesus without believing in his Resurrection?
2. 'To accept Jesus as Lord is to submit to a fundamental change in our values and our life-style.' Do you agree?
3. Does the contemporary emphasis on personal freedom and individual rights militate against the call to confess Jesus as Lord and to live in obedience to his commands?
4. The unique quality of the lordship of Jesus is revealed in his humility. In the above painting of the resurrected Christ by William Blake (c.1795)[19], the figure of Jesus does not express triumphalism or worldly glory, but a quiet and self-effacing tenderness as he shows his disciples the marks of the nails in his hands and feet. What does this painting tell us about the nature of the lordship of Jesus?

Jesus Christ Today

CONCLUSION

After a summary of the main points of the discussion the group should compose itself for the closing time of prayer and one member should read the words of dedication from the Covenant Service of the Methodist Church [20]:

> I am no longer my own, but yours.
> Put me to what you will,
> rank me with whom you will;
> put me to doing, put me to suffering;
> let me be employed for you or laid aside for you,
> exalted for you or brought low for you;
> let me be full, let me be empty;
> let me have all things, let me have nothing;
> I freely and wholeheartedly yield all things
> to your pleasure and disposal.
> And now, glorious and blessed God,
> Father, Son and Holy Spirit,
> you are mine and I am yours.
> So be it.
> And the covenant now made on earth,
> let it be ratified in heaven. Amen.

Jesus Christ Today

After a space for prayer the group to read together:

> *Lord Jesus Christ,*
> *set us under your lordship.*
> *Sanctify us in your service,*
> *make us faithful in our stewardship,*
> *humble in our dealings with others,*
> *bold in our stand for justice,*
> *constant in prayer,*
> *and joyful and earnest in our witness to you. Amen.*

Hymn: 'Lord of all hopefulness, Lord of all joy' (C.H. 92).

THE BENEDICTION.

Jesus Christ Today

STUDY 8

JESUS, THE WAY

AIM

To explore the description of Jesus as the Way and to consider how Jesus informs and directs our Christian faith and witness today.

WELCOME AND OPENING PRAYER
Hymn: *'Thou art the Way: to thee alone'* (C.H. 121) and brief opening prayer.

STARTING POINT
The late W. E. Sangster once referred in a sermon to a London church badly damaged in the blitz and boarded up. A notice fixed to the main door of the church read, 'This building is not an air-raid shelter!' Sangster went on to warn against *hideaway* religion, a haven that offered escape from the harsh realities of life, within the safety of creeds, rituals and changeless traditions. The Bible, on the other hand, invites us to embark on a *highway*, to set out in obedience on the way of Christ, to discover new patterns of witness and service, and to be open to new experiences and insights.

Jesus said *'I am the Way.'* He does not offer us shelter within safe traditional structures, but calls us to walk his Way – a way that leads to a fuller knowledge of God, to the discovery of new values, to a promise of new life and a vision of a new heaven and a new earth. But Jesus does not simply point us to the way, he is the way and he is our companion on the journey.

Centuries before Jesus the Psalmist had prayed, *'Teach me your way, O Lord'* (Ps. 27:11). Moses feared that after his death people would abandon the way which he had taught them: *'For I know that after my death you will surely act corruptly, turning aside from the way that I have commanded you. In time to come trouble will befall you, because you will do what is evil in the sight of the Lord* (Deut. 31: 29). Through Isaiah God directed his people to the

Jesus Christ Today

way of holiness and obedience to his laws: *'And when you turn to the right or when you turn to the left, your ears shall hear a word behind you, saying, "This is the way; walk in it"'* (Isa. 30: 21).

But the claim of Jesus goes beyond the Old Testament directive to walk in God's way. Jesus did not say, 'I will show you the way,' but rather, *'I am the Way.'* The heart of Christian faith and life lie, not in the teachings of Jesus, but in his person and in a living relationship to him. It is in him that we discover what God is like. It is in him that we experience reconciliation to God. It is he who leads us to understand the precepts and values of life in the kingdom. The way of Jesus is the way of truth and revelation, of grace and salvation, of faith and holiness. His moral and ethical teaching cannot be separated from his revelation of God or from the new relation to God made possible through his life, death and resurrection. Together they constitute the Christian adventure in which we are called to participate in the company of our Lord.

C.S.Lewis ends his spiritual autobiography, *Surprised by Joy* [21], by comparing the experience of becoming a Christian to that of discovering a way out of a wood:

'When we are lost in the woods the sight of a signpost is a great matter. He who first sees it cries, "Look!" The whole party gathers round and stares. But when we have found the road and are passing signposts every few miles, we shall not stop and stare. They will encourage us... but we shall not stop and stare, or not much; not on this road, though their pillars are of silver and their lettering of gold. "We would be at Jerusalem."'

What other signposts today try to draw us away from the way of Christ?

BIBLE STUDY

Following his promise of rooms in his Father's house Jesus answered Thomas' question about the way he would take to go to the Father by saying that he himself was the way to God, adding that he too was *'the truth and the life.'*

Jesus Christ Today

"'If I go and prepare a place for you, I will come again and will take you to myself, so that where I am, there you may be also. And you know the way to the place where I am going." Thomas said to him, "Lord, we do not know where you are going. How can we know the way?" Jesus said to him, " I am the way, and the truth, and the life. No one comes to the Father except by me. If you know me, you will know my Father also. From now on you do know him and have seen him."' (John 14: 3 – 7).

In the Book of Acts we hear of Apollos who had been taught the Way of the Lord, but on his arrival in Ephesus it became clear that he required more instruction in the faith:

'Now there came to Ephesus a Jew named Apollos, a native of Alexandria. He was an eloquent man, well-versed in the scriptures. He had been instructed in the Way of the Lord; and he spoke with burning enthusiasm and taught accurately the things concerning Jesus, though he knew only the baptism of John. He began to speak boldly in the synagogue; but when Priscilla and Aquila heard him, they took him aside and explained the Way of God to him more accurately.' (Acts 18: 24 – 26).

The Letter to the Hebrews speaks of Jesus, through his death on the cross, opening up a new way to the Father:

'Therefore, my friends, since we have confidence to enter the sanctuary by the blood of Jesus, by the new and living way that he opened for us through the curtain (that is, through his flesh), and since we have a great priest over the house of God, let us approach with a true heart in full assurance of faith, with our hearts sprinkled clean from an evil conscience and our bodies washed with pure water' (Hebrews 10: 19-22).

As the way of Jesus led for him to death on a cross, those who walk his way have also encountered suffering and persecution. According to his own confession before the court in Jerusalem, Paul, before his conversion, had persecuted those who walked the way of Christ:

"I am a Jew, born in Tarsus in Cilicia, but brought up in this city at the feet of Gamaliel, educated strictly according to our ancestral law,

Jesus Christ Today

being zealous for God, just as all of you are today. I persecuted this Way up to the point of death by binding both men and women and putting them in prison, as the high priest and whole council of elders can testify about me'" (Acts 22: 3 – 5)

On the basis of these passages we see that Jesus is the Way in the sense that he leads us to God and to fullness of life in this world and in heaven. In following him and walking in his way his disciples make him known to others, and consequently Christian faith and life became known as *'The Way'* and the followers of Jesus as *'those of the Way.'* Because the way of Christ challenged the precepts and outlook of the authorities of his day, he encountered scorn, hostility and eventually death on the cross. Subsequently, his followers too were persecuted. To this day the way of Christ – the way of justice, peace and compassion – finds itself in confrontation with the unjust, oppressive and violent ways of the world.

DISCUSSION

1. Is it sufficient to describe Christianity as 'a way of life'?
2. 'Walking the way of Christ calls for both *faith* and *action* – faith in God as he has been revealed in Jesus Christ and active conformity to the life made known in Jesus.'
   Discuss.
3. Would it be fair to say that the failure of Christians to walk the way of Christ is the greatest obstacle to others recognising and accepting his way?
4. The above drawing by Rolando Zapata from Mexico is entitled *The Power of the Powerless* (1976)[22]. Oppressive political power is contrasted to the power of tenderness and vulnerability. The cross itself is not to be seen, but the crucified Jesus is recognised by a child. What does this picture say to us about the conflict between the way of Christ and the way of violence and oppression today?

Jesus Christ Today

CONCLUSION

After a brief summing up of the discussion George Herbert's Poem, 'The Call,'[23] should be read by a member of the group:

> *Come, my Way, my Truth, my Life:*
> *Such a Way, as gives us breath:*
> *Such a Truth, as ends all strife:*
> *And such a Life, as killeth death.*
>
> *Come, my Light, my Feast, my Strength:*
> *Such a Light, as shows a feast:*
> *Such a Feast, as mends in length:*
> *Such a Strength, as makes his guest.*
>
> *Come my Joy, my Love, my Heart:*
> *Such a Joy, as none can move:*
> *Such a Love, as none can part:*
> *Such a Heart, as joys in love.*

A short time of silence and prayer to be concluded with the group saying together:

> *Lord Jesus Christ,*
> *you said that you are the Way, the Truth, and the Life:*
> *keep us from straying from you, for you are the Way,*
> *from distrusting your promises, for you are the Truth,*
> *and from resting in any other thing than you, for you are the Life.*
> *By your Holy Spirit,*
> *teach us what to believe,*
> *what to do,*
> *and wherein to take our rest;*
> *for your name's sake. Amen.*

Hymn: 'Show me thy ways, O Lord' (C.H.74).

THE BENEDICTION

Jesus Christ, For Ever

STUDY 9

JESUS, HEAD OF THE CHURCH

AIM

In this third section of our studies we turn to those aspects of the person and work of Jesus which relate particularly to the future. We begin with the image of Jesus as the head of the church and consider the meaning and significance of this title for the life of the church today.

WELCOME AND OPENING DEVOTIONS
Hymn: *'Christ is made the sure foundation'* (C.H. 10) and opening prayer.

STARTING POINT
This ancient Christian hymn, translated and adapted by J. M. Neale, links together three images of Jesus – as the foundation, the head and the cornerstone of the church. It is he who calls his church into being, binds his people in unity, and inspires their praise and their witness. But is this image of the church in its relation to Jesus meaningful for us today?

'Jesus – Yes! The Church – No!' So read the title of a pamphlet published in connection with an evangelical campaign. The appeal of the person and teaching of Jesus remains even in this secularized age, but the popular image of the church is that of empty and decaying buildings, small and aged congregations, meaningless denominational divisions, irrelevant activities and an insipid and ineffectual leadership.

One reason for the decline evidenced in the life of the church today is that people find it difficult to associate the radical message and person of Jesus of Nazareth with the dreariness and lifelessness of religious institutions. David Watson wrote that the church that preaches the gospel must *embody* the gospel in its worship, its relationships and its joy.

Jesus Christ, For Ever

For the writers of the New Testament it was impossible to think of Jesus without thinking of the church, or to think of the church without thinking of Jesus. This is reflected in the images used to describe the church: *The People of God, God's Building, The Fellowship of the Spirit, The Household of Faith, The Bride of the Lamb, The Body of Christ.* In each of these metaphors the human structures *(people, building, fellowship, family, body, etc)* are closely allied to God, Christ, the Spirit and faith. One of the highest and most significant images is that of *The Body of Christ.* In developing the implications of this concept Paul emphasizes the place and the role of every member within the body, with Jesus Christ as its head.

The activities of the body are determined by the head. Similarly, in the church, the whole body responds to the control of the head and bows to his rule. As there can be no head without a body, so it follows that Christ is present in the unity of the head and the body. Although a literal identification of Jesus with the Church has to be avoided, it remains true that he is present in the life and being of the church, which is sanctified and motivated by his life. To the degree in which the church is open in obedience to the direction of Christ its head, he makes himself known and becomes active in the world through his church.

Hans Küng, the Roman Catholic theologian, explains the significance of the relation of the body to the head in his book, *The Church* [24]:

'Christ gives himself to the church, but he is never wholly contained in it. Christ is the head, and he remains the head, which controls the body. The concept of head always carries overtones of the ruler. The body can exist only in total dependence on him. It is of vital importance for the church that it allows Christ to be its head; otherwise it cannot be his body... The church remains constantly and in all things dependent on Christ, in every moment of its existence, and constantly needs his grace and forgiveness... Given that Christ is the head of the church and hence the origin and goal of its growth, growth is only possible in obedience to the head. If the church is disobedient

Jesus Christ, For Ever

to its head and his word, it cannot grow, however busy and active it may seem to be, it can only wither.'

What does obedience to the head mean in practice in the day-to-day life of the church?

BIBLE STUDY

Paul claims that God has set Jesus in a position of authority over all things, in this present age and in the age to come, and has also made him head over all things in the church:

'**He has put all things under his feet and has made him the head over all things for the church, which is his body, the fullness of him who fills all in all**' (Ephesians 1: 22-23).

Rather than be drawn to every false doctrine and worldly ideology, God's people should follow the truth as it has been revealed in Jesus and grow in his likeness. In so doing, the whole body will grow and every part will be built up in love:

'**We must no longer be children, tossed to and fro and blown about by every wind of doctrine, by people's trickery, by their craftiness in deceitful scheming. But speaking the truth in love, we must grow up in every way into him who is the head, into Christ, from whom the whole body, joined and knitted together by every ligament with which it is equipped, as each part is working properly, promotes the body's growth in building itself up in love**' (Ephesians 4: 14-16).

A similar emphasis is found in the Letter to the Colossians. Believers are safeguarded from the effects of false teaching and the body will grow and prosper, to the extent in which believers remain constant in their faithfulness to Christ the head:

'**The substance belongs to Christ. Do not let anyone disqualify you, insisting on self-abasement and worship of angels, dwelling on**

Jesus Christ, For Ever

visions, puffed up without cause by a human way of thinking, and not holding fast to the head, from whom the whole body, nourished and held together by its ligaments and sinews, grows with a growth that is from God' (Colossians 2: 17-19).

Each of the above extracts from Paul's Letters points us to different aspects of the relation between Jesus and his church:

– Jesus is set by God as head of the church, as he has been raised above all creation. His headship is not confined to the church. It follows that the task of the church is to lead the world to recognize, to acknowledge and to extoll Jesus as head.
– The use of the images of head and body to describe Jesus and the church emphasize the close relation between them. The same life flows through both the head and the body, and as all members of the church are members of the body of Christ, it follows that his life fills, directs and empowers the whole body.
– As head, Jesus is Lord of the church and the final authority over its life. The first responsibility of the church is to be open to the will of its Lord and to obey him.
– Obedience to the head is the condition of the church's growth, the source and inspiration of which lie, not in human effort and achievement, but in the divine life reflected in Jesus, which flows in and through the church, building it up in love, faith and witness.

Jesus Christ, For Ever

DISCUSSION

1. Are we in danger, in the life of the church, of placing custom, denominational tradition, confessions of faith, constitution and order, or the personal influence of leaders, above the primary authority of Jesus, the head?
2. If Jesus is head and if his life flows in and through the church, why do so many churches today wither and decline?
3. How does a local congregation discover what is the mind and purpose of Christ for its life and witness?
4. When Llandaff Cathedral was restored following the damage inflicted to the building in the Second World War, the huge bronze statue of Christ by Epstein entitled *Majestas* [25], above, was set on a concrete arch across the nave. Does the statue and its location succeed in conveying the sense of Christ as head of the church?

Jesus Christ, For Ever

CONCLUSION

Following a brief summing up of the discussion a member of the group should read the following extract from 'Prayers for Pilgrims' by John Johansen-Berg [26]:

> *Are you like a wisp of straw,*
> *carried this way and that by every puff of wind?*
> *Or are you like a growing plant,*
> *firmly rooted in the ground,*
> *able to withstand harsh winds*
> *and growing ever upwards towards God?*
> *To use another image,*
> *you are part of a body*
> *which finds its strength and direction*
> *from Jesus Christ, the head.*
> *This body grows and becomes strong through love.*
> *So we are within a fellowship,*
> *always ready to speak the truth, yet doing so with love,*
> *that our unity may be maintained*
> *and the body continue to grow.*
> *Is this the nature of the fellowship to which you belong?*
> *Is Christ truly the head of the body?*
> *Is there a caring unity for the good of all?*

Jesus Christ, For Ever

Time of prayer, to be concluded by saying together

> *Lord Jesus, we are your church on earth:*
> *possessed and empowered by you;*
> *you are the source of our life and our hope,*
> *of our faith and our endeavour,*
> *of our strength and our vision.*
> *Claim us, make us wholly yours,*
> *and use us to accomplish your purpose*
> *and to extend your kingdom in the world. Amen*

Hymn: 'Jesus, with thy church abide' (C.H. 490).

THE BENEDICTION

Jesus Christ, For Ever

STUDY 10

THE COSMIC CHRIST

AIM

To explore the connection in the New Testament between Jesus, creation and nature, and to consider the implications of belief in the Cosmic Christ for the Christian attitude to the created order and the environment today.

WELCOME AND OPENING DEVOTIONS

Hymn: *'Eternal Ruler of the ceaseless round'* (C.H. 514) and brief opening prayer.

STARTING POINT

The opening words of the Bible read, *'In the beginning God created the heavens and the earth.'* The first sentence of the Apostles' Creed reads, *'I believe in God, the Father Almighty, Maker of heaven and earth'* – words which echo the first verse of Genesis, but with one difference: God the creator is also described as the *Father Almighty*. Christian faith insists that the God who created all things is the same as the God who revealed himself in Jesus Christ. The creator is also the saviour. And there are important reasons for holding together these two aspects of the work of God.

Jesus Christ, For Ever

The Bible is clear that the world came into being, not by accident, but as the action of a wise, holy and loving God. Nonetheless, one problem has continued to haunt religious people from the dawn of history, namely, the presence of evil in the world. What is the source of evil? Was evil purposely created by God? If so, he cannot be regarded as good. Or was evil the result of a flaw in God's creation? If so, he cannot be almighty. In the early years of Christianity a group of thinkers known as *Gnostics* attempted to solve the dilemma. One school of Gnostics claimed that creation was not the work of God, but of inferior and imperfect divine beings, or emanations. Other Gnostics propounded the theory that the world had been created by the cruel and vindictive God of the Old Testament, not the holy and loving God and Father of the Lord Jesus Christ.

Faced with this dangerous dualism and the idea of two gods in conflict with one another, the writers of the New Testament were anxious to show that the God who had redeemed the world in Jesus Christ was also the God who had created the world in the first place. If God had acted in Jesus to save the world, and if Jesus was the eternal Word of God who became flesh, then it followed that the incarnate Word was one and the same as the creative Word which had brought all things into being at

Jesus Christ, For Ever

the beginning of time. The world had been created through the Son in the first place, and the world had now been recreated through the Son, through his death and resurrection. Both creation and redemption were the work of the same God, at work through his Son, and in the power of his Spirit. The New Testament writers then took one further step in their reasoning. If all things came into being through Jesus, and all things are redeemed through Jesus, then Jesus is Lord of all and in the fullness of time all things will be brought to their final completion in him.

The reflections and conclusions of Paul and other New Testament authors on the significance of the Cosmic Christ were not merely an exercise in abstract theology nor were they simply an attempt to solve an intellectual problem which bothered first century thinkers. The belief that Jesus is the source, the saviour, and the Lord of creation, leads us to understand our relationship to the natural world and to the environment and our responsibility to co-operate with him in protecting and saving the world.

In the following passage from his spiritual diary, *Cudd fy Meiau* [27], Dr. Pennar Davies sees the life of Christ shining through all creation, despite the growth of towns, industries and the threat of pollution:

Jesus Christ, For Ever

'The Lord of the Resurrection is everywhere; in every living particle, every fireball, every unit of energy, every void.

I had the opportunity today to look at a vast view. Apart from the sea and the clouds and the sky there was none of nature's beauty in it; a large town with its industries and houses, and beyond it, the greyish sea, mist, cloud and the tender immensity of the sky; little men and their limited, raw busyness, and around them the stupefying abundance of the whole world; chattering, grunting, smiling sardonically and mouthing, and around everything all the excellence of the limitless mercy. And I felt that we were not worthy of the Christ who is in the creation. Every movement, every breathing, every crystallizing, every response to sun and shadow – is not the same power here as in the resurrection?'

Does the awareness of the life of Christ pulsating through all creation deepen our sense of responsibility to protect the environment?

Jesus Christ, For Ever

BIBLE STUDY

For the author of John's Gospel, to believe in Jesus as the Word of God made flesh is also to believe that all things were created through him:

'In the beginning was the Word, and the Word was with God, and the word was God. He was in the beginning with God. All things came into being through him, and without him not one thing came into being. What has come into being in him was life, and the life was the light of all people' (John 1: 1-4).

In his Letter to the Colossians, Paul takes the concept of Christ in creation a step further. If all things were created through Christ, it follows that he is head over all and all things are reconciled and are held in being in him:

'He is the image of the invisible god, the firstborn of all creation; for in him all things in heaven and on earth were created, things visible and invisible, whether thrones, or dominions or rulers or powers – all things have been recreated through him and for him. He himself is before all things, and in him all things hold together. He is the head of the body, the church; he is the beginning, the firstborn from the dead, so that he might come to have first place in everything. For in him all the fullness of God was pleased to dwell, and through him God was pleased to reconcile to himself all things, whether on earth or in heaven, by making peace through the blood of his cross' (Colossians 1: 15-20).

Jesus Christ, For Ever

According to the Letter to the Hebrews, the Son, through whom all things have been created, shares the nature and glory of God:

'In these last days he (God) has spoken to us by a Son, whom he appointed heir of all things, through whom he also created the worlds. He is the reflection of God's glory and the exact imprint of God's very being, and he sustains all things by his powerful word. When he had made purification for sins, he sat down at the right hand of the Majesty on high' (Hebrews 1: 2-3).

The meaning of *firstborn* in Colossians 1:15 is first in honour, or first in eminence. As the *firstborn from the dead*, Christ, who existed in the beginning with God, is eternal, above time, and consequently beyond the control of death and the grave. The concept of the Cosmic Christ contains important insights for our understanding of the person of Jesus.

- The God who has revealed himself in Jesus as our loving heavenly Father is also the creator God who made the world and the worlds.
- The divine Word by which all things were made in the beginning is also the Word that became flesh in the man, Jesus of Nazareth, in order to deal with the problem of evil and through his death and resurrection to reconcile the world to God.
- The love and power of the divine Word in Jesus Christ, which permeates and sustains the whole of creation, will, in the end, bring all things to completion.
- The task of Christians and the church is to bear witness to the life of Christ which sustains the created world, to protect the variety and richness of creation, and to proclaim and demonstrate his reconciliation of all things to God.

Jesus Christ, For Ever

DISCUSSION

1. What does it mean to say that Jesus has reconciled the whole of Creation to God?

2. Has Christian teaching traditionally emphasized individual salvation and neglected the cosmic dimension of Christ's redemptive work? What were the consequent effects on our attitude to nature and the environment?

3. What are the practical implications of the church's witness to the work of Christ in creation for the present ecological crisis?

4. The above painting by the contemporary artist, Frank Hendrey, is entitled, *Christ in the Cosmos* [28]. What does the figure of Christ set in space with outstretched arms convey? Does the painting add to our understanding of the Cosmic Christ?

Jesus Christ, For Ever

CONCLUSION

After a brief summing up of the discussion a member of the group should read part of Psalm 8:

> *When I look at your heavens, the work of your fingers,*
> *the moon and the stars that you have established:*
> *what are human beings that you are mindful of them,*
> *mortals that you care for them?*
>   *Yet you have made them a little lower than God,*
> *and crowned them with glory and honour.*
>   *You have given them dominion over the works of your hands;*
> *you have put all things under their feet,*
> *all sheep and oxen, and also the beasts of the field,*
> *the birds of the air, and the fish of the sea,*
> *whatever passes along the paths of the sea.*
>   *O Lord, our Sovereign,*
> *how majestic is your name in all the earth!*

Jesus Christ, For Ever

Silence and time for prayer and reflection to be concluded by saying together:

> *For the Word and the Power,*
> *creating, sustaining and renewing all things,*
> *we give you thanks, O God.*
> *For creating us in your own image,*
> *and endowing us with skills and understanding;*
> *for the ability to recognize good and evil,*
> *and for the wisdom to choose between them:*
> *we give you thanks, O God.*
> *For creating us as one human family,*
> *for calling us to love and care for one another,*
> *for surrounding us with the rich and fruitful resources of the earth,*
> *and for charging us with the responsibility of caring for your world:*
> *we thank you, O God. Amen.*

Hymn: 'Lord of light, whose Name outshineth' (C.H. 510).

THE BENEDICTION

Jesus Christ, For Ever

STUDY 11

CHRIST THE JUDGE

AIM
To explore the sense in which the New Testament portrays Jesus as judge and to consider the place and significance of judgement within Christian faith and life today;

WELCOME AND OPENING DEVOTIONS
Hymn: *'Lo! he comes, with clouds descending'* (C.H. 316) and opening prayer.

STARTING POINT
Charles Wesley's portrayal in his hymn of Christ returning in glory on the clouds of heaven may seem to us unfamiliar and problematic. Is there a place in contemporary Christianity for the concept of Christ the judge? Two significant facts are worth noting in Wesley's picture of Jesus' return. The first is that the Christ who comes to judge is the same as the Christ who died on the cross as saviour; his body still bears the tokens of his passion. Secondly, his return is an occasion of praise and triumph, not of terror and dread.

The Weiskirche in the village of Weis bei Neugaden in Bavaria, an eighteenth century rococo church which has been described as the most beautiful village church in the world, contains a mural depicting Christ the judge by the artist Johann Zimmermann. Like Charles Wesley, he portrays Jesus returning as judge in glory and sitting on a rainbow, the sign of forgiveness and of a new covenant. With his right hand he points to the cross, and with his left hand to the wounds in his side and to his heart, the sign of love. This image is consistent with the emphasis of the New

Jesus Christ, For Ever

Testament. The Christ who returns is not a cruel and vindictive judge, but the same Christ who came to reconcile the world to God.

All religions that make moral and ethical demands and emphasize obedience to the commands of God, responsibility towards other people and the practice of justice, mercy, and peace in human relationships, invariably emphasize the concept of accountability and judgement. All ethical religion is based on obedience to the dictates of God, and on man's responsibility before God, particularly with regard to his response to the needs of the poor and the destitute. These themes figure prominently in the parables of Jesus. The master punishes the unforgiving servant because of his vindictive behaviour towards a fellow servant (Matt. 18: 21-35). In the parable of the talents the man judged and punished is the one who fails to make creative use of the gift given to him by God (Matt. 25: 14-30). And in the same chapter the nations are judged for their failure to meet the needs of the hungry, the oppressed, the sick and the deprived (Matt. 25 31-46). Luke's Gospel gives us the account of the judgement of the rich man who ignored the needs of Lazarus the beggar (Luke 16: 19-31).

Jesus condemns the money-changers in the Temple for their dishonest dealings and their contempt for the house of God. He judged the Pharisees for their lack of concern for the poor and for placing greater store on religious convention than on human compassion. Our inclination is to be angry when we ourselves have been abused or unfairly treated. But Jesus was angry when he saw injustice towards others, human rights being flouted and the things of God being misused. Jesus responded with righteous indignation to the oppression of the poor and the hypocrisy of the self-righteous.

To experience judgement is to stand before Christ and to feel his holiness exposing our sin and unworthiness, awakening our sense of guilt, and driving us to our knees in repentance and supplication. In his book, *Windows on the Cross* [29], Tom Smail emphasizes that judgement inevitably

Jesus Christ, For Ever

follows egotism and sin, but the final goal of God's justice is not condemnation but mercy:

'When human nature becomes self-centred rather than God-centred, when we set ourselves up as manufacturers of our own lifestyles and begin to ignore the Maker's instructions, there is in personal and social life conducted in that way an inbuilt destructiveness that sets people into life-eroding and ultimately fatal conflicts with one another, with their environment and internally with themselves... The judgments of God do not mainly consist of his directing at us supernatural thunderbolts from heaven. To condemn sin he only needs to stand back and let us have our own way, because if we are left to ourselves, we shall destroy ourselves without his having to do anything about it. The judgement of God consists in letting sinful human nature have its own way and devise its own destruction... But the final goal of God's justice can never be condemnation; it is at its very heart saving justice, it is the means by which he asserts his mercy on behalf of those who are most in need of it.'

The objective of Jesus the judge is not primarily to condemn but to save. Do you agree?

BIBLE STUDY

In his sermon in the house of Cornelius Peter says that God has commanded them as apostles to affirm that Jesus Christ is the one appointed by God to be judge of all:

'He commanded us to preach to the people and to testify that he is the one ordained by God as judge of the living and the dead. All the prophets testify about him that everyone who believes in him receives forgiveness of sins through his name' (Acts 10: 42-43).

According to Paul the responsibility of believers is to live in a manner pleasing to the Lord, remembering that they must appear before the judgement seat of Christ:

Jesus Christ, For Ever

'So whether we are at home or away, we make it our aim to please him. For all of us must appear before the judgement seat of Christ, so that each may receive recompense for what has been done in the body, whether good or evil' (2 Cor. 5:9-10).

In calling on his readers to be patient in their dealings with one another James reminds them that the second coming of the Lord is near and the judge is standing at the door:

'You must also be patient. Strengthen your hearts, for the coming of the Lord is near. Beloved, do not grumble against one another, so that you may not be judged. See the Judge is standing at the doors!' (James 5: 8-9).

According to John's Gospel the Father gave authority to judge to the Son:

'"The Father judges no one but has given all judgement to the Son, so that all may honour the Son just as they honour the Father. Anyone who does not honour the Son does not honour the Father who sent him... And he has given him authority to execute judgement, because he is the Son of Man. Do not be astonished at this; for the hour is coming when all who are in their graves will hear his voice and will come out – those who have done good to the resurrection of life, and those who have done evil to the resurrection of condemnation"' (John 5: 22-23, 27-30).

Although all are judged by the words of Jesus, he did not come into the world to judge but to save:

'"I do not judge anyone who hears my words and does not keep them, for I came not to judge the world, but to save the world. The one who rejects me and does not receive my word has a judge; on the last day the word that I have spoken will serve as judge"' (John 12: 47-48).

Jesus Christ, For Ever

Jesus came into the world primarily to reveal the love of the Father and to reconcile the world to him. At the same time the light of his holy love exposes the horror of human sinfulness and awakens a sense of guilt. That is the experience of judgement. Although the New Testament often associates judgement with the second coming of Jesus or with the hour of death, nonetheless every encounter with Christ is a moment of judgement. His person, his teaching and his example bring judgement to bear on our impure thoughts, our cruel words, our egotistical motives, our indifference to the needs and sorrows of the poor, our lack of faith, our spiritual poverty and every other sin that stains our souls. The precepts of the kingdom are a constant judgement on all injustice and oppression, on every occasion of conflict and violence, on every situation of hunger and economic deprivation, on every abuse of human rights. His righteous indignation shames and humbles us, and inspires us to work to further his kingdom of peace and justice on earth.

DISCUSSION

1. What difference does it make to our concept of judgement to remember that Jesus our judge is also our loving saviour?
2. In what sense is every encounter with Christ a moment of judgement?
3. What factors in modern life and in our scientific and technological culture incline people to reject the concept of judgement?
4. The above portrayal of the angry Christ is the work of Lino Pontepon[30]. Does he succeed in conveying the sense of righteous indignation? What is the difference between fury, rage and righteous anger? Bearing in mind that the artist is an Asian Christian, why do you think he chose to depict Jesus in this way?

Jesus Christ, For Ever

CONCLUSION

The main points of the discussion to be summed up and a member of the group to read the following poem by Edmund Banyard [31].

Edmund Banyard describes a man on trial under an oppressive regime. He has neither the education or the fluency to defend himself effectively, but he imagines what he would like to be able to say:

*'I am condemned because your law
allows no place for me.
My crimes I freely admit:
I am homeless, seeking shelter
where I may rear my family in modest decency.
I am stateless, seeking a country
where I may belong by right in God's good earth.
I am destitute, claiming a share of the wealth
that is our common heritage.
I am a sinner, needing aid from fellow sinners.*

*You will dispose of me according to your law,
but you will not so easily dispose of him
who owns me, citizen of his kingdom.
He frowns on crimes your law condones:
pride, selfishness and greed,
self-righteousness, the worship of all things material,
and the refusal to acknowledge me as a brother.*

*By your law I stand condemned;
but one day you must answer to the master of us all
for the havoc caused by your law in his realm.'*

Jesus Christ, For Ever

A time for prayer and silence, followed by a prayer to be read by all:

*Lord Jesus, we praise you for revealing to us
your compassion, your mercy and your grace:
compassion which is stronger than all the hatred of the world;
mercy which overcomes all our sins;
grace which melts the hardness of our hearts.
In you we trust, for in you is our hope. Amen.*

Hymn: *'O Thou, my Judge and King'* (C. H. 666)

THE BENEDICTION.

Jesus Christ, For Ever

STUDY 12

CHRIST, ALPHA AND OMEGA

AIM
To explore the meaning of the phrase 'Alpha and Omega' as a title for Jesus, and to consider its relevance for our understanding of time and the turn of the Millennium.

WELCOME AND OPENING DEVOTIONS
Hymn: *'God is working his purpose out'* (C.H. 303) and opening prayer.

STARTING POINT
Alpha is the first letter of the Greek alphabet and *Omega* is the last. Both letters were used by Jews and Greeks to represent God and to designate the beginning and the end of time. According to Greek thinkers God was the beginning of all things because he was the creator and in him all things had their origin. He was the end because all things moved towards him and came to their completion in him. He was the centre because all things existed in him and had their being in him.

A similar concept is found in the Old Testament. The Prophet Isaiah hears God saying to him *'I, the Lord, am first, and will be the last'* (Isaiah 41:4). What is surprising is that a phrase, used exclusively to speak of God, came to be used in the Book of Revelation to describe Jesus. The God who is the first and the last, the beginning and the end, is the God who is revealed in Jesus Christ and who is at work in the world through him.

The concept of Christ as Alpha and Omega points us to the meaning and purpose of *time*. In the Bible, time is more than the passage of minutes, hours, days and years. Time is God's creation and gift to humankind. It has its source and its beginning in God, and it will come to an end when all

Jesus Christ, For Ever

things come to their completion in Christ. And because time has its beginning and its end in the purpose of God, that in turn gives significance to the present. It is in the present moment that God meets and challenges us. Paul, quoting from the prophecy of Isaiah, says *'Now is the acceptable time; see, now is the day of salvation'* (2 Corinthians 6:2; c.f. Isaiah 49:8).

If time is part of God's creation, it follows that the course of history is under his rule. The Old Testament Prophets saw the hand of God in the political events of their day. They believed that the divine purpose was being worked out in the affairs of nations and would ultimately be brought by God to their fulfilment in judgement and salvation. The relation between time and the growth of the kingdom of God is understood in similar terms in the New Testament. In Jesus the kingdom has been inaugurated, and yet the kingdom is still to come in its fullness at the end of time.

What is true of the course of history and of the progress of the kingdom is also true of our individual lives. Having lost his possessions and his sons and daughters, Job declares, *'Naked I came from my mother's womb, and naked shall I return there; the Lord gave, and the Lord has taken away; blessed be the name of the Lord'* (Job 1:21). As we have come from God, so shall we return to God.

In his *Ecclesiastical History of the English Nation* [32], the Venerable Bede (673-735 A.D.) tells the story of the Christian missionary, Paulinus, preaching before King Edwin of Northumbria. Having ended his sermon the king turned to his counsellors and asked for their opinion of this new faith. One of the king's chief men responded

'The present life of man, O king, seems to me, in comparison with that time which is unknown to us, like to the swift flight of a sparrow through the room wherein you sit at supper in winter... The sparrow, flying in at one door and immediately out at another, whilst he is within is safe from the wintry tempest. But after a short space he immediately vanishes out of your sight, passing from winter into winter again. So this life of man appears for a short space, but of what went before and of what is to follow

Jesus Christ, For Ever

we know nothing at all. If, therefore, this new doctrine contains something more certain on the beginning and end of life, it justly deserves to be followed.'

'Without Christ, human life is little more than meaningless existence between the darkness of birth and the darkness of death' (Helmut Thielicke). Do you agree?

BIBLE STUDY

While speaking of God redeeming his people from bondage in Babylon, Isaiah declares that God is the *first* and the *last*, who existed before time and human history, and who will remain changeless when all else has passed away:

'Thus says the Lord, the King of Israel and his Redeemer, the Lord of hosts: "I am the first and I am the last; besides me there is no god"' (Isaiah 44:6).

The phrase *Alpha and Omega* is used three times in the Book of Revelation, twice in relation to God and once as a description of the Lord Jesus Christ. John, the author of Revelation, claims that his visions were granted to him by God:

'"I am the Alpha and the Omega," says the Lord God, who is and who was and who is to come, the Almighty' (Revelation 1:8).

'And the one who was seated on the throne said, "See, I am making all things new." Also he said, "Write this, for these words are trustworthy and true." Then he said to me, "It is done! I am the Alpha and the Omega, the beginning and the end"' (Revelation 21:5-6).

Speaking of his second coming Jesus says to John:

'"See, I am coming soon; my reward is with me, to repay according to everyone's work. I am the Alpha and the Omega, the first and the last, the beginning and the end"' (Revelation 22: 12-13).

Jesus Christ, For Ever

The words *first* and *last*, *beginning* and *end*, as translations of *Alpha and Omega*, are capable of a double meaning. They can mean first and last in point of time. This means that Christ the Son was before the world began and will be when the world is ended. But they can also mean beginning and end in the sense of *source* or *origin* and *goal* and *consummation*. This then means that the divine Word, which became flesh in Jesus Christ, is the source and origin of life and time, and the goal and end of all things to which life and time move. He is the creator of life and in him life comes to its perfection and ultimate fulfilment. As we have come from him, so shall we return to him.

DISCUSSION

1. Does the belief that time and history have their origin in God and are moving towards their ultimate fulfilment in him, give a special significance to the approach of the new Millennium?
2. 'To say that Jesus Christ is Alpha and Omega is also to say that love is the origin and final goal of life.' Do you agree?
3. How should we today understand the concept of the second coming of Christ?
4. The above picture is of a mural in the catacomb of Commodilla[33], to the south of Rome. Dating from the fourth century, it is one of the earliest portraits of Jesus in existence. He is shown with the letters Alpha and Omega symbolizing that he is the begining and end of human life. Bearing in mind its age and that it appears on the wall of a catacomb, what does this picture tell us about the meaning of death?

Jesus Christ, For Ever

CONCLUSION

After a summing up of the discussion the group should compose itself as a member reads

> *Father of love*
> *source of life and breath,*
> *creator of heaven and earth,*
> *giver of food and drink,*
> *of warmth and clothing*
> *and life in all its rich and varied beauty:*
> > *You are Alpha and Omega*
> > *the beginning and end of all things.*
>
> *Word of God made flesh,*
> *friend of the poor,*
> *one of us and yet one with God,*
> *crucified and risen,*
> *bringing all things to their completion:*
> > *You are Alpha and Omega*
> > *the first and the last.*
>
> *Wind and breathe of God,*
> *unfathomable energy of life,*
> *bringing order out of chaos,*
> *disturbing and comforting,*
> *reviving and reforming,*
> *invisible, yet filling all things:*
> > *You are Alpha and Omega,*
> > *with the Father and the Son, one God,*
> > *from beginning to end and to all eternity*

Jesus Christ, For Ever

Time for prayer and silence to end with all saying together the Cafod Millennium Prayer:

*God of all ages, Lord of all time,
you are the Alpha and the Omega,
the origin and goal of everything that lives,
yet you are ever close to those
who call on you in faith.*

*We look with expectant joy
to the Jubilee of your Son's coming among us,
two thousand years ago.
We thank you for the years of favour
with which you have blessed your people.
Teach us to share justly the good things
which come from your loving hand;
to bring peace and reconciliation
where strife and discord reign;
to speak out as advocates
for those who have no voice;
and to rejoice in a bond of prayer and praise
with our sisters and brothers throughout the world.*

*When Christ comes again in glory
may he find us alive and active in faith,
and so call us to that kingdom
where, with you and the Holy Spirit,
he is God, to be praised, worshipped and glorified,
both now and for ages to come. Amen.*

Jesus Christ, For Ever

Hymn: *'Now thank we all our God'* (C.H. 368).

THE BENEDICTION

Sources

Sources

1. Brendan O'Malley (Editor), *A Welsh Pilgrim's Manual*, Gomer, Llandysul, 1989
2. Willis S. Wheatley, *'Jesus Christ, Liberator,'* Division of Mission, United Church of Canada, from *Risk*, Vol. II Nos. 2-3, World Council of Churches, Geneva, 1975.
3. John Macquarrie, *The Humility of God*, SCM Press, London. 1978.
4. Jaroslav Pelikan, *Jesus Through the Centuries*, Yale, 1985.
5. Marc Chagall, *'The White Crucifixion,'* 1938, The Art Institute of Chicago, from J. Pelikan (ibid).
6. Norman Mailer, *The Gospel According to the Son*, Abacus, London, 1997.
7. Morris Maddocks, *The Christian Healing Ministry*, S.P.C.K., London, 1990.
8. Giovanni Meloni, *'Gesu Medico,'* Galleria d'Arte Sacra Contemporanea, Assisi, from *Risk* (op. cit.).
9. J. Cameron Peddie, *'The Forgotten Talent,'* Fontana, London and Glasgow, 1966.
10. William Temple, *Readings in St. John's Gospel*, Macmillan, London, 1939.
11. Ford Madox Brown, *'Jesus Washing the Feet of Peter,'* The Tate Gallery, London, from Nancy Grubb, *The Life of Christ in Art*, Artabras, London, 1996.
12. Janet Morley (Editor), *Bread of Tomorrow*, S.P.C.K. and Christian Aid, London, 1992.
13. El Greco, *'The Saviour'*, c. 1610-14, Museo Del Greco, Toledo, from J. Pelikan (op.cit.).

Sources

14. Albert Schweitzer, *The Quest of the Historical Jesus*, A & C. Black, London 1922.
15. Richard Bennett, *Blynyddoedd Cynnar Methodistiaeth*, Caernarfon, 1909, (tr.).
16. Guido Rocha, *'The Tortured Christ,'* 1975, All Africa Conference of Churches Training Centre, Nairobi, from Hans-Ruedi Weber, *On a Friday Noon*, S.P.C.K., London, 1979.
17. Sheila Cassidy, *Light from the Dark Valley*, DLT, London, 1994.
18. Oscar Romero and Jon Sobrino, *Romero: Martyr for Liberty*, Catholic Institute for International Relations, London, 1982.
19. William Blake, *'Christ Appearing to the Apostles after the Resurrection,'* c.1795, Yale Centre for British Art, from J. Pelikan (op.cit.).
20. *The Methodist Service Book*, Methodist Publishing House, London, 1975.
21. C. S. Lewis, *Surprised by Joy*, Geoffrey Bles, London, 1955.
22. Rolando Zapata, *'The Power of the Powerless,'* 1976, Private Collection, Geneva, from Hans-Ruedi Weber (ob.cit.).
23. Robert Van de Weyer, *The Harper Collins Book of Prayers*, Castle Books, Edison, New Jersey, 1997.
24. Hans Küng, *The Church*, Burn and Oates, London, 1967.
25. Epstein, *Majestas*, Llandaff Cathedral, by permission.
26. John Johansen-Berg, *Prayers for Pilgrims*, DLT, London, 1993.
27. Brendan O'Malley (op.cit.).
28. Frank Hendrey, *'Christ in the Cosmos,'* Static Gallery, Roscoe Lane, Liverpool.
29. Tom Smail, *Windows on the Cross*, DLT, London, 1995.
30. Lino Pontebon, *'The Angry Christ,'* Asian Christian Art Association, from Masao Takenaka and Ron O'Grady, *The Bible Through Asian Eyes*.

Sources

31. Geoffrey Duncan, *Dare to Dream,* Fount, London, 1995.
32. Bede, *The Ecclesiastical History* of the *English Nation,* Everyman, J. M. Dent, London, 1916.
33. *'Christ in Majesty, with Alpha and Omega,'* (C.4th) from catacomb in Commodilla, to the south of Rome, from John Macmanners, *The Oxford Illustrated History of Christianity,* Oxford, 1990.